D1551477

Best Easy Day Hikes
Flagstaff

Help Us Keep This Guide Up to Date

Every effort has been made by the author and editors to make this guide as accurate and useful as possible. However, many things can change after a guide is published—trails are rerouted, regulations change, facilities come under new management, etc.

We would love to hear from you concerning your experiences with this guide and how you feel it could be improved and kept up to date. While we may not be able to respond to all comments and suggestions, we'll take them to heart and we'll also make certain to share them with the authors. Please send your comments and suggestions to the following address:

> The Globe Pequot Press
> Reader Response/Editorial Department
> P.O. Box 480
> Guilford, CT 06437

Or you may e-mail us at:

> editorial@GlobePequot.com

Thanks for your input, and happy trails!

FALCONGUIDES®

Best Easy Day Hikes Series

Best Easy Day Hikes
Flagstaff

Second Edition

Bruce Grubbs

FALCONGUIDES®

GUILFORD, CONNECTICUT
HELENA, MONTANA

AN IMPRINT OF THE GLOBE PEQUOT PRESS

FALCONGUIDES®

Library of Congress Cataloging-in-Publica-
tion Data is on file.
ISBN 978-0-7627-5106-8

Printed in the United States of America

10 9 8 7 6 5 4 3 2 1

Contents

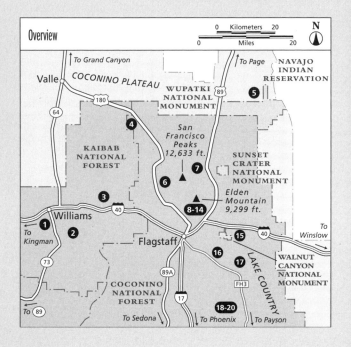

Overview

0   Kilometers   20
0   Miles   20

N

To Grand Canyon

Valle

COCONINO PLATEAU

To Page

NAVAJO
INDIAN
RESERVATION

180

64

④

WUPATKI
NATIONAL
MONUMENT

89

⑤

KAIBAB
NATIONAL
FOREST

San
Francisco
Peaks
12,633 ft.

⑦

▲

⑥

③

40

Williams

To
Kingman

①

②

73

Flagstaff

SUNSET
CRATER
NATIONAL
MONUMENT

Elden
Mountain
9,299 ft.

▲

8-14

⑮

40

To
Winslow

⑯

⑰

WALNUT
CANYON
NATIONAL
MONUMENT

89A

COCONINO
NATIONAL
FOREST

LAKE COUNTRY

FH3

To (89)

17

18-20

To Sedona

To Phoenix

To Payson

Acknowledgments

I would like to thank my many hiking companions over the years, who have put up with my incessant trail mapping and photography. Thanks to Duart Martin for her support and encouragement. And finally, thanks to my editors at The Globe Pequot Press, Scott Adams, Jan Cronan, and Josh Rosenberg, for making a book out of my rough manuscript.

Ranking the Hikes

Although all of the hikes in this book are relatively easy, some are longer and have more elevation change than others. To help you decide which hike works best for you, I have provided below a list of all the hikes ranked from easiest to most challenging.

Introduction

Visitors arriving in the Flagstaff area are often surprised to find themselves in a beautiful, green forest in the middle of what is commonly thought of as desert country. High peaks, often snow-capped, tower above the forested plateau, and the cool mountain air beckons the traveler to stay a while. Surely such a landscape must have some fine trails to hike. It does indeed—and this book is your ticket to the easiest and most accessible day hikes in the area.

Flagstaff, a small city of about 60,000 residents, lies on the southern section of the Colorado Plateau, a vast area of high desert and forested mountains that encompasses most of northern Arizona and southern Utah, as well as portions of Colorado and New Mexico. The public lands of the Coconino National Forest surround the city, and the Kaibab National Forest adjoins the Coconino National Forest to the west. Horizontal layers of sedimentary rocks—mostly sandstone, shale, and limestone—underlie the plateau, and lava flows darken the plateau's surface here and there. Hundreds of volcanic mountains and cinder cones, some over 12,000 feet in elevation, dot the landscape. There are several designated wilderness areas in the region, and an expanding network of urban trails connects Flagstaff to the surrounding Forest Service trail system.

During the summer and fall, when most people visit Flagstaff, the climate is mild and inviting. Daytime high temperatures average in the mid-80s F at 7,000 feet, and are cooler at higher elevations. Summer nights are chilly, with temperatures dropping into the 50s or even 40s F. Summer thunderstorms may brew up in the afternoons, but the rain showers soon pass and the moisture helps bring out the mountain wildflowers.

Crisp fall days are delightful for hiking, and the mountain slopes are slashed with gold as the aspen trees change color in anticipation of the winter to come. Daytime high temperatures in autumn are in the 70s F, but nights can be quite chilly, often dipping below freezing by dawn.

The first heavy snowfall usually comes in late November or in December, and the Flagstaff area is often snow covered until March or April. Winters are highly variable. In dry years many of the hikes in this book can be done in midwinter. Snowstorms commonly last a day or two, and are followed by several days or a week of clear, dry weather. See the section on "Road and Trail Conditions" later in the introduction for a list of trails that dry out soon after a storm.

This pocket-sized book contains a selection of the easiest day hikes from my more comprehensive FalconGuides, *Hiking Northern Arizona* and *Hiking Arizona*. This book should serve as an introduction to day hiking in the Flagstaff area for those with limited time, or for those who prefer easier hikes. These hikes provide a generous sample of the great hiking we enjoy in northern Arizona. The twenty hikes described here range from 1 to 14 miles in length. Most of the hikes are just a few miles long and have gentle gradients and moderate elevation changes. All of the hikes are on established, easy-to-follow trails.

Zero Impact

Despite its sometimes lush appearance, northern Arizona is a dry region. It can take dozens to hundreds of years to recover from damage done by humans. Soils in this high plateau region are thin and easily eroded. Evidence of ignorant and careless recreational use is all too evident along forest roads in the form of litter, trampled campsites, and massive fire rings. Fortunately, most backcountry users are better informed and more conscientious than vehicle-based recreationists are, and most trail sides reflect this care. A few simple guidelines will help you leave the land and the trail as you found it.

Waste
Pack out all garbage and trash. If you can carry items in when they are full, you can carry them out empty. After your hike, dispose of trash at trailhead receptacles, if available, or in waste containers at a campground, rest area, or other facility.

Do not feed wild animals—human food is very bad for them, and animals that become used to human handouts lose their fear of humans and become nuisances that may have to be killed.

Human waste must be disposed of carefully or it becomes a health hazard. Select a site at least 100 yards from streams, lakes, springs, and dry washes. Avoid barren, sandy soil, if possible. Next, dig a small "cat-hole" about six inches down into the organic layer of the soil.

Some people carry a small plastic trowel for this purpose. When finished, refill the hole, and make the site look as natural as possible. Land managers now recommend that all toilet paper be carried out. Use double zipper bags with a small amount of baking soda to absorb odor.

Stay on the Trail
Do not cut switchbacks or take other shortcuts. This practice erodes trails, increases the cost of trail maintenance, and

requires you to expend more energy than if you stay on the trail. The ground in many areas is fragile. Soil takes a long time to form in alpine meadows and pinyon-juniper forest, and plants have a tenuous foothold. Avoid walking off trail in such areas if possible. When traveling cross-country, stay on pine needles, rock, sand, or gravel as much as you can, and spread your group out to avoid creating a new trail. Never construct tree blazes, rock cairns, or any other type of trail marker.

Archaeological Sites

The Sinagua (Spanish for "without water") people occupied the Flagstaff region approximately 1,000 years ago, and many of their ruins and artifacts are scattered throughout the area. Fine examples are preserved at Wupatki National Monument, near the Doney Trail hike, and at Walnut Canyon National Monument, near the Walnut Canyon Rim hike. Please treat all ruins and artifacts with respect, no matter where you find them. Stay off walls and structures, and leave all artifacts in place. Many ruins in the area have yet to be studied by archaeologists. A great deal of information can be gained by studying tools, potsherds, chipping sites, and other remains in their original context. If such artifacts are moved or disturbed, an important part of the puzzle is destroyed forever. Rock art such as pictographs and petroglyphs is especially fragile. These rock drawings and carvings have survived hundreds or thousands of years because the climate is relatively dry. Skin oils can quickly degrade the pigments used in rock paintings, so please resist the urge to touch any rock art.

The best way to enjoy ancient ruins and artifacts is from a distance. Take nothing but photographs. The Federal

Antiquities Act protects both prehistoric and historic ruins and artifacts. If you observe anyone illegally excavating or disturbing a site, please report him or her to the nearest national forest ranger station at the phone number listed in the hike description.

Three Falcon Zero-Impact Principles

- Leave with everything you brought.
- Leave no sign of your visit.
- Leave the landscape as you found it.

Play It Safe

Although some of the trails in this book are very near urban areas, others are more remote. In either case, you should be prepared for any weather and trail conditions you might encounter. These hikes range in elevation from 6,000 to 10,000 feet. If you normally reside at low elevations, take it easy in the thin mountain air until your body has had time to acclimatize. This process can take several days.

Maps

The hikes in this book are easy to follow, and maps are provided showing details of each trail, so you don't need to buy extra maps. On the other hand, more detailed maps are essential if you decide to explore farther or go off trail. All of the hikes in this book are covered by the detailed topographic maps published by the U.S. Geological Survey, which are available through local outdoor shops or from the Survey at (888) ASK-USGS or http://store.usgs.gov/.

The entire area described in *Best Easy Day Hikes Flagstaff* is covered by the Coconino National Forest and Kaibab National Forest maps. These maps are available from the ranger stations listed in each hike description, as well as from bookstores and outdoor shops. The national forest maps show the forest road network and are useful for finding trailheads and general orientation.

Another map option is the excellent computer-based coverage of the Flagstaff area found on Topo Arizona, published by National Geographic Maps, 3212 Beaver Brook Canyon Road, Evergreen, CO 80439; (800) 962-1643; maps@ngs.org, www.natgeomaps.com.

Water

Although elevations are high and the air is often cool, this is a dry climate. Dehydration begins slowly and its effects are insidious. Prolonged dehydration leads to heat exhaustion and eventually to sunstroke, a life-threatening medical emergency. Even if your condition does not become this serious, thirst and dehydration will take the fun out of your hike. Always carry at least one quart of water per person. During May and June, or on longer hikes, you may need two or more quarts per person. Do not count on finding water on any hike. If you use natural water sources, remember that all water should be treated with a water purification system before consumption. It is easier and safer to carry all the water you will need from home or town.

Sun

The sun is intense in the Flagstaff area because of the southerly latitude and high elevations. Wear protective clothing and especially a sun hat. Use a sunscreen lotion with a sun protection factor of at least 45 for maximum protection against sunburn and the aging effects of sunlight. A tan does not make you immune to sunburn!

Cold

Though summers are usually pleasant, snow may fall during any time of year, especially on the San Francisco Peaks. (Officially named San Francisco Mountain, the locals call this collection of 11- to 12,000-foot summits the "San Francisco Peaks," or just "the Peaks.") During the summer rainy season (July through mid-September), thundershowers can lower the temperature from the dry and comfortable 70s F to the wet and chilling 40s F in a matter of minutes. Carry rain gear and an extra layer of warmth, such as a polyester fleece top. Fall weather is almost always delightful during the day, but the nights are cold, and the temperature often dips well below freezing. Be prepared with windproof outer layers, warm gloves, and a hat.

Dogs

Dogs are allowed on all the trails in this book, but city ordinances require that they must be on a leash within city limits. In the national forests, you must keep your dog under control, either by leash or by training. If your dog barks, runs up to other hikers, or chases wildlife, it is not under control and should be left at home. Uncontrolled dogs give dogs and their owners a bad name.

Road and Trail Conditions

Most of the trails and their access roads are open by May, and the first winter rain and snow rarely comes before November. Snow and mud make most forest roads impassable during the winter. To avoid costly road damage from vehicles, the Forest Service often closes back roads until they dry out in the spring. Heavy rains from thunderstorms can make a road or trail temporarily impassable, even in summer. There are a number of trails accessible from paved trailheads, and some trails dry out more rapidly than others after wet weather. Good wet weather or off-season trails are: Red Mountain (Hike 4), Doney Trail (Hike 5), Rocky Ridge Trail (Hike 9), Fatmans Loop (Hike 11), Buffalo Park (Hike 13), Observatory Mesa Trail (Hike 14), and Mormon Lake (Hike 18). For the latest conditions, check with the Forest Service ranger station listed in the appropriate hike description.

Flash floods occur when a sudden rain dumps a lot of water onto a small area. This can occur during the summer thunderstorm season or during winter when a warm storm drops rain onto the snowpack. Normally dry washes and drainages can fill with water in a matter of seconds. Stay out of narrow canyons when thunderstorms threaten.

Never attempt to drive across a flooded wash. The road-bed may be washed out and the depth may be greater than you think. Less than 1 foot of swift-moving water can wash a vehicle away.

Hike Plan

Always tell a reliable person your hiking plans, especially if you will be hiking in the more remote areas. On the hike, stick to your plan, and afterward, be sure to check back in with that same person. Rescue teams get a bit irritated when they discover the person they have been looking for all night has been asleep in bed all that time.

The Coconino County sheriff is responsible for search and rescue in this area. Dial 911 for emergency assistance.

Cellular Phones

Cell phone coverage is pretty good in the Flagstaff area, but coverage is spotty in the more remote areas, especially in the canyons. Do not let a cell phone replace common sense and preparedness. Carry appropriate water, food, and clothing for the expected conditions. Backcountry rescues take hours to organize, and you will probably be forced to spend the night out before rescuers can reach you.

Gear Every Hiker Should Carry

- Water
- Food
- Sun hat
- Sunscreen
- Sunglasses
- Durable hiking shoes or boots
- Synthetic fleece jacket or pullover
- Rain gear
- Map
- Compass
- First-aid kit
- Signal mirror
- Toilet paper and zippered plastic bags

Map Legend

══⟨90⟩══	Interstate highway
══⟨30⟩══	U.S. highway
══⟨20⟩══	State highway
══⟨41⟩══	Local/Forest Roads
＝ ＝ ＝ ＝	Unimproved/Gravel road
- - - - - - -	Trail
▪▪▪▪▪▪▪	Featured route
· · · · · · · · ·	Cross country route
——————	River/Creek
— · · — · ·	Intermittent stream
⬭	Lake
▭	National Forest
⬚	National Monument
⬚	Indian reservation
⏝	Bridge
▲	Campground
⊥⊥⊥⊥⊥⊥⊥	Cliffs
□	Road exits
ⵏ	Gate
🅿	Parking
⤳	Pass
▲	Peak
🏕	Picnic area
■	Point of interest/other trailhead
📷	Ranger station
⌁	Spring
❻	Trailhead
∬	Waterfall
🔲	Viewpoint
N ⬇	True North (Magnetic North is approximately 15.5° East)

Williams

The town of Williams is on the southwest corner of the Coconino Plateau at the north base of Bill Williams Mountain. Although the Coconino Plateau was part of New Spain for 300 years, the Spanish had little to do with the area. American mountain men such as Bill Williams were the first to put the Coconino Plateau on the modern map. When much of Arizona was ceded to the United States in 1848, American exploration naturally increased. Wagon roads were pushed through the area, and in 1883 the coming of the railroad made northern Arizona easier to reach. A spur track was built from Williams to the south rim of the Grand Canyon, replacing the torturous stage ride with a comfortable train trip. Tourism blossomed, and Williams became known as the "Gateway to the Grand Canyon."

The small mountain town is surrounded by the ponderosa pine forests of Kaibab National Forest, which offers many enjoyable hikes. Extinct volcanoes and cinder cones, steep-sided, symmetrically shaped volcanoes formed when magma under high pressure erupts explosively, relieve the otherwise flat surface of the plateau; the hikes described in this section take advantage of these features.

Camping

A number of public campgrounds are in the Kaibab National Forest in the Williams area. Cataract Lake Campground is just west of town off Interstate 40. Kaibab Lake Campground is a few miles north of town on Highway 64 and Forest Road 47. Dogtown Lake Campground is south on the Perkinsville Road (Coconino County 73), and east on Forest Road 140 and Forest Road 132. The Dogtown Lake Trail starts from this campground. Another popular campground is located at White Horse Lake, which is south of Williams on Coconino County 73 and east on Forest Roads 110 and 14. Private campgrounds include KOA Grand Canyon, and KOA Williams–Grand Canyon, both north of town on Highway 64. Unless specifically posted otherwise, dispersed camping is allowed in the Kaibab National Forest. Be extremely careful with fire, especially during the summer and fall dry seasons. Campfires are prohibited during periods of high fire danger.

Access and Services

The Williams area is accessed from either east or west via I-40, and from the north via Highway 64. Most services are available in Williams.

1 Buckskinner Trail

This is an easy trail that starts from Buckskinner Park in the town of Williams. It can be used as the short, easy hike described here, or as part of a more ambitious hike by connecting to the Bill Williams Trail.

Location: In Williams.
Distance: 2 miles out and back.
Approximate hiking time: 1 hour.
Elevation change: 200 feet.
Best seasons: Late spring through fall.
Water: Water is available at Clover Spring. Be sure to treat the water before drinking.
Other trail users: Horses and mountain bikes.

Canine compatibility: Dogs are allowed if kept under control.
Permits and restrictions: None.
Maps: USGS Williams South; Kaibab National Forest (Williams and Tusayan Ranger Districts).
Trail contacts: Williams Ranger District, Kaibab National Forest, 742 South Clover Road, Williams, AZ 86046, (928) 635-5600, www.fs.fed.us/r3/kai/.

Finding the trailhead: From Route 66, Williams's main street, turn south on 4th Street. Go two blocks, then turn right (west) on Sherman Avenue. After two more blocks, turn left (south) onto 6th Street. Follow this street a short distance out of town. Keep left (south) at the Forest Service complex, and follow 6th Street (now maintained dirt) to Buckskinner Park, which is on the right (west) just before the end of the road at City Reservoir. The trailhead is behind the ramadas to the west.

The Hike

This well-defined trail heads south-southwest into a ravine,

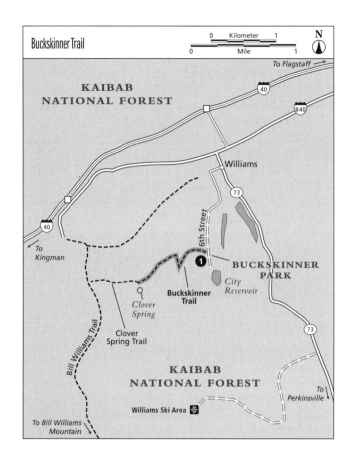

then works its way to the top of a volcanic terrace. A few Douglas firs mix with the ponderosa pine–Gambel oak forest, but when the trail reaches the flatter terrain above, the firs disappear. The trail continues west-southwest, crosses another ravine, and reaches Clover Spring at 1 mile. This is a logical turnaround point for a short, easy hike.

For a longer hike, continue on Clover Spring Trail for 0.5 mile to Bill Williams Trail, then turn left (south) to hike to the top of Bill Williams Mountain. This is a climb of more than 2,000 feet, and adds 6 miles to the round-trip distance. *Hiking Northern Arizona* includes more information on the Bill Williams Trail.

Miles and Directions

0.0 Trailhead at Buckskinner Park.

1.0 Reach Clover Spring, your turnaround point.

2.0 Arrive back at the trailhead.

2 Dogtown Lake Trail

This is an easy walk around the shores of Dogtown Lake, a small but scenic reservoir set in the beautiful ponderosa pine forest southeast of Williams.

Location: 7 miles southeast of Williams.

Distance: 1.8-mile loop.

Approximate hiking time: 1 hour.

Elevation change: None.

Best seasons: Late spring through fall.

Water: Water is available from Dogtown Lake. Treat the water before drinking.

Other trail users: Horses and mountain bikes.

Canine compatibility: Dogs are allowed if kept under control.

Permits and restrictions: None.

Maps: USGS Williams South; Kaibab National Forest (Williams and Tusayan Ranger Districts).

Trail contacts: Williams Ranger District, Kaibab National Forest, 742 South Clover Road, Williams, AZ 86046, (928) 635-5600, www.fs.fed.us/r3/kai/.

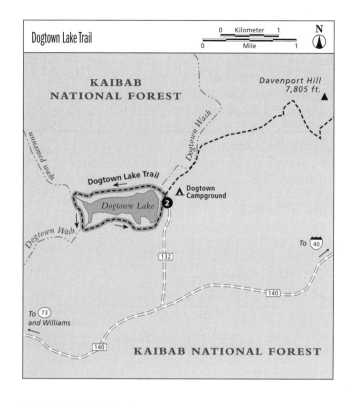

Dogtown Lake Trail

0 Kilometer 1

0 Mile 1

N

KAIBAB
NATIONAL FOREST

Davenport Hill
7,805 ft.

Dogtown Wash

unnamed wash

Dogtown Lake Trail

Dogtown
Campground

Dogtown Lake

2

Dogtown Wash

To 40

132

140

To 73
and Williams

140

KAIBAB NATIONAL FOREST

Finding the trailhead: From Williams, drive 3.9 miles south on 4th Street (Coconino County 73), then turn left (east) on Forest Road 140. Follow this maintained dirt road for 3 miles, then turn left (north) onto maintained Forest Road 132. Continue 1 mile to Dogtown Campground. Bear left into the campground and use the trailhead parking near the boat ramp.

The Hike

This is an easy, pleasant walk through the pine forest along the Dogtown Lake shore. Head north from the trailhead to walk the loop counterclockwise. At 0.7 mile, at the northwest corner of the lake, cross an unnamed, normally dry wash that empties into the lake. Dogtown Wash, at the southwest side of the lake, is the main inlet to the lake. You will cross this at 1.0 mile. Like most streambeds on the Coconino Plateau, these washes carry water only when the snow melts in early spring, and intermittently thereafter following heavy summer thunderstorms.

Continue on the trail until you loop back to the trailhead at 1.8 miles.

Miles and Directions

0.0 Trailhead at Dogtown Lake.
0.7 Reach the unnamed wash.
1.0 Pass the Dogtown Wash.
1.8 Return to the trailhead.

3 Keyhole Sink Trail

This very easy trail leads to a unique petroglyph site located in a box canyon near Sitgreaves Mountain. The pleasant walk takes you through stands of pine and aspen.

Location: 11 miles east of Williams.

Distance: 2 miles out and back.

Approximate hiking time: 1 hour.

Elevation change: 100 feet.

Best seasons: Spring through fall.

Water: None.

Other trail users: Horses and mountain bikes.

Canine compatibility: Dogs are allowed if kept under control.

Permits and restrictions: None.

Maps: USGS Sitgreaves Mountain; Kaibab National Forest (Williams and Tusayan Ranger Districts).

Trail contacts: Williams Ranger District, Kaibab National Forest, 742 South Clover Road, Williams, AZ 86046, (928) 635-5600, www.fs.fed.us/r3/kai/.

Finding the trailhead: From Williams, drive east on Interstate 40 about 8 miles to the Pittman Valley Road exit. Cross the interstate to the north, then turn right (east) on old Route 66. Continue for 2 miles to the Oak Hill Snowplay Area parking lot, which is on the right (south).

The Hike

The trail (which is not shown on the topographic map) starts at a gate on the north side of the road. The trail descends very gradually through an open ponderosa pine forest and small meadows, then turns northeast and passes a small stand of aspen before ending in a box canyon at the Keyhole Sink at 1 mile. A rail fence, interpretive sign, and visitors' register

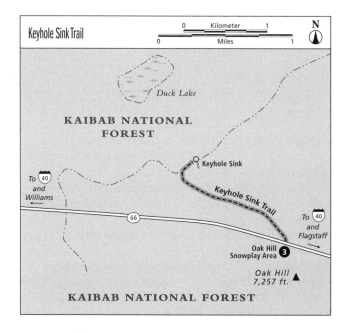

Kilometer

0   Miles   1

N

Duck Lake

**KAIBAB NATIONAL
FOREST**

Keyhole Sink

Keyhole Sink Trail

To 40
and
Williams

66

To 40
and
Flagstaff

Oak Hill
Snowplay Area 3

Oak Hill
7,257 ft. ▲

KAIBAB NATIONAL FOREST

mark the spot. The low, colorful volcanic cliffs, the aspens and pines, and the pool of water all combine to make this a pleasant spot, especially in the late afternoon.

Look carefully, and you will find a number of petro-glyphs along the base of the wall. One of these clearly depicts a herd of deer entering the canyon. Usually the exact meaning of this ancient rock art is more elusive. Please do not touch or otherwise disturb the petroglyphs; they are protected by federal law as a fragile link to the unwritten past. Such artwork is one of the few signs of pre-historic human habitation still found in this section of the Coconino Plateau. Although it is likely that early hunting parties passed through this area from time to time, the short growing season and the lack of water probably discouraged permanent settlement.

Miles and Directions

0.0 Trailhead.

1.0 Reach Keyhole Sink, your turnaround point.

2.0 Arrive back at the trailhead.

Coconino Plateau

The Coconino Plateau is the southernmost portion of the Colorado Plateau, and covers the region surrounding the San Francisco Peaks, north of the Mogollon Rim and south of the Grand Canyon. Several hundred cinder cones and old volcanoes dot the area, ranging in elevation from 8,000 to 12,633 feet. The hikes in this section explore these old volcanic features. The Kendrick Mountain and the Kachina Peaks Wilderness Areas also are on the Coconino Plateau.

Camping

Bonito Campground is the only public campground in this area. It is located near Sunset Crater National Monument, off U.S. Highway 89 on Forest Road 545. Dispersed camping is allowed in the Coconino National Forest unless specifically posted otherwise. Be extremely careful with fire, especially during the summer and fall dry seasons. Campfires are prohibited during periods of high fire danger.

Access and Services

Access to the western portion of the plateau is via U.S. Highway 180, which runs across the west slopes of the San Francisco Peaks from Flagstaff to the Grand Canyon. The eastern portion of the plateau is reached from US 89, which runs north from Flagstaff and passes east of the San Francisco Peaks. Interstate 40 runs east to west through Flagstaff and crosses the southern sections of the plateau. Flagstaff is the largest city in the area, and all services are available here.

4 Red Mountain

Follow a short trail to a colorful, highly eroded volcanic mountain on the Coconino Plateau. Easy walking through pinyon pine and juniper woodland leads to a small but fantastically eroded canyon full of stone hoodoos and other weird formations.

Location: 31 miles northwest of Flagstaff.
Distance: 2.8 miles out and back.
Approximate hiking time: 2 hours.
Elevation change: 150 feet.
Best seasons: Spring through fall.
Water: None.
Other trail users: None.

Canine compatibility: Dogs are allowed if kept under control.
Permits and restrictions: None.
Maps: USGS Chapel Mountain; Coconino National Forest.
Trail contacts: Peaks Ranger District, Coconino National Forest, 5075 N. Highway 89, Flagstaff, AZ 86004, (928) 526-0866, www.fs.fed.us/r3/coconino/.

Finding the trailhead: From Flagstaff, drive 31 miles north on U.S. Highway 180, then turn left (west) on the signed Red Mountain Trailhead road. Continue 0.3 mile to the trailhead.

The Hike

From the trailhead, the Red Mountain Trail passes through several clearings in the pinyon-juniper forest, offering tantalizing views of Red Mountain. After dropping into a drainage, the trail follows this gully directly toward Red Mountain. A stone wall, probably built as a dam, marks the entrance to the badlands. Use the wooden stairs to surmount

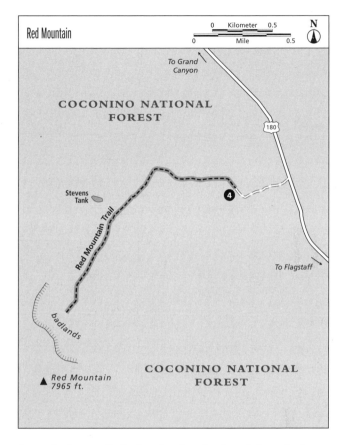

the wall, then walk the last few hundred yards into the heart
of the reddish badlands. Return as you came.

Miles and Directions

0.0 Trailhead.

1.4 Reach the volcanic badlands.

2.8 Arrive back at the trailhead.

5 Doney Trail

This very easy, short walk to the top of a volcanic cinder cone near Wupatki National Monument features an extensive view of the Painted Desert, including lava flows and the distant San Francisco Peaks.

Location: 39 miles northeast of Flagstaff.
Distance: 1 mile out and back.
Approximate hiking time: 1 hour.
Elevation change: 200 feet.
Best seasons: All year.
Water: None.
Other trail users: Horses and mountain bikes.

Canine compatibility: Dogs are allowed if kept under control.
Permits and restrictions: None.
Maps: USGS Wupatki SW.
Trail contacts: Peaks Ranger District, Coconino National Forest, 5075 N. Highway 89, Flagstaff, AZ 86004, (928) 526-0866, www.fs.fed.us/r3/coconino/.

Finding the trailhead: From Flagstaff, drive north about 30 miles on U.S. Highway 89, then turn right (east) at the signed Wupatki National Monument Road (Forest Road 545). Follow this paved road east for 9.2 miles, then turn right (southeast) at the signed picnic area and park at the signed trailhead.

The Hike

This broad, easy trail heads south toward the low saddle between two cinder cones. From the saddle, you can take a 100-yard walk to the left (north) for a view from the lower cinder cone. Back on the main trail, continue south about 0.4 mile to the summit at 0.5 mile. The 360-degree view includes sweeping vistas of the Painted Desert. The

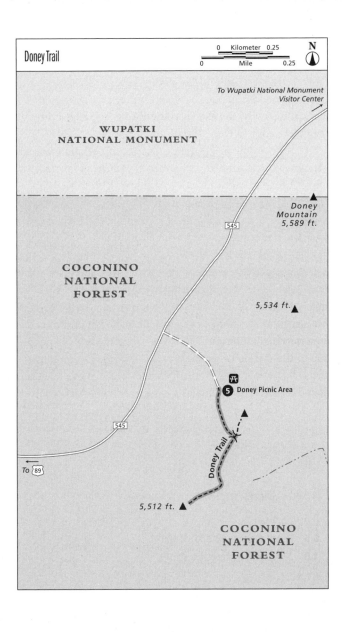

Doney Trail

0   Kilometer   0.25

0   Mile   0.25

N

To Wupatki National Monument
Visitor Center

WUPATKI
NATIONAL MONUMENT

Doney
Mountain
5,589 ft.

545

COCONINO
NATIONAL
FOREST

5,534 ft.

Doney Picnic Area
5

Doney Trail

545

To 89

5,512 ft.

COCONINO
NATIONAL
FOREST

soft, rounded slopes, bluffs, and mesa in the distance to the northeast were formed when the soft, pastel-colored shale eroded away. At noon, the harsh, vertical light gives the Painted Desert a washed-out, dull look. In contrast, when the sun is low in the sky in late evening or early morning, the colors come alive.

The area to the north and east is part of Wupatki National Monument, established to preserve numerous prehistoric ruins. After the initial eruption of Sunset Crater Volcano in A.D. 1065, the natives living in the Wupatki area were forced to abandon their homes and fields because of the rain of volcanic ash and cinders. A few years later, however, the people discovered that the thin layer of ash acted as a mulch to retain soil moisture, allowing them to grow crops in many new areas. The result was a population explosion in the Wupatki area. Members of the Sinagua culture from the south, the Anasazi from the northeast, and Cohonina people from the west migrated to the area. The three cultures advanced rapidly due to the sharing of technology and increased social interaction. However, by 1225, the Wupatki area was mostly abandoned. A fifty-year drought that began in 1150 was probably a contributing factor. The profound impact makes one think about the effects such a prolonged dry period would have on our desert civilization.

Retrace your steps to return to the trailhead.

Miles and Directions

0.0 Trailhead.
0.5 Reach the summit and viewpoint.
1.0 Arrive back at the trailhead.

San Francisco Peaks

The San Francisco Peaks are the highest mountains in Arizona, culminating in 12,633-foot Humphreys Peak. A horseshoe-shaped ring of peaks surrounds the 10,000-foot Interior Valley, which opens to the northeast. Like all the smaller mountains and hills on the Coconino Plateau, the San Francisco Peaks are the remnants of an ancient volcano. Many geologists believe that the mountain once reached 16,000 feet or more. There is evidence that the mountain exploded in a violent volcanic eruption much like the one at Mount St. Helens in Washington in 1980. After the explosion, the Interior Valley, a classic U-shaped valley, was carved by glacial ice. As recently as 10,000 years ago, glaciers were present in the Interior Valley and in the northeast canyons. Glacial features can be seen on several of the hikes. Most of the San Francisco Peaks are protected in the Kachina Peaks Wilderness Area.

In 1889, C. Hart Merriam, a biologist with the U.S. Biological Survey, camped at Little Spring on the northwest slope of the San Francisco Peaks. He came to study the great variety of plant life that grew on the mountain and the surrounding plateau. He soon noticed that plants tended to grow in associations determined by climate. The climate grows cooler and wetter as the elevation increases because the high terrain extracts more rain and snow from storm clouds. Merriam determined that a 1,000-foot elevation gain is approximately equivalent to 600 miles of northward travel in terms of climate and ecosystems. Groups of plants grow at elevations where the climate is amenable. Animals dependent on certain plants for food are also associated with these plant communities. Merriam invented the term "life zone" to describe such plant and animal communities, and first described the characteristic life zones of northern Arizona.

Although later studies have complicated the life zone model, it is still a useful way to understand the plant and animal communities of the Southwest. If you were to travel from the Colorado River at the bottom of the Grand Canyon to the top of the San Francisco Peaks, you would gain more than 10,000 feet of elevation in 52 miles, and pass through life zones equivalent to those found on a horizontal journey from northern Mexico to northern Canada.

Hiking on the mountain is somewhat restricted. The Interior Valley forms part of a watershed for the city of Flagstaff and is closed to overnight camping. Day hiking is allowed. All of the region above 11,400 feet (the approximate elevation of timberline) is closed to cross-country hiking and hikers must stay on designated trails. This closure was implemented to protect the San Francisco Peaks groundsel (*Senecio franciscanus*), an endangered plant that is found nowhere else on the planet. For closure information, contact the Forest Service Peaks Ranger District at (928) 526-0866.

Camping

Bonito Campground is the only public campground in this

area. It is located off U.S. Highway 89 on Forest Road 545 near Sunset Crater National Monument. Dispersed camping is allowed in the Coconino National Forest unless specifically posted otherwise. Be extremely careful with fire, especially during the summer and fall dry seasons. Campfires are prohibited during periods of high fire danger.

Access and Services

U.S. Highway 180 skirts the west slopes of the San Francisco Peaks, running northwest from Flagstaff. The Arizona Snowbowl Road, 7 miles northwest of Flagstaff off US 180, is the highest paved access road on the mountain. The east slopes are reached from US 89, north of Flagstaff. The nearest services are in Flagstaff.

6 Kachina Trail

This relatively new trail offers an easy hike through a gor-geous mixed alpine forest of ponderosa pine, limber pine, Douglas fir, and quaking aspen, as well as scenic alpine meadows. The hike is on the southwest slopes of the San Francisco Peaks, in the Kachina Peaks Wilderness Area.

Location: 14 miles northwest of Flagstaff.
Distance: 5.4 miles out and back.
Approximate hiking time: 3 hours.
Elevation change: 400 feet.
Best seasons: Summer through fall.
Water: None.
Other trail users: Horses.
Canine compatibility: Dogs are allowed if kept under control.

Permits and restrictions: Cross-country hiking is prohibited above 11,400 feet (approximately timberline). Camping is not allowed above Lockett Meadow in the Interior Valley.
Maps: USGS Humphreys Peak; Coconino National Forest.
Trail contacts: Peaks Ranger District, Coconino National Forest, 5075 N. Highway 89, Flagstaff, AZ 86004, (928) 526-0866, www.fs.fed.us/r3/coconino/.

Finding the trailhead: From Flagstaff, drive northwest on U.S. Highway 180 about 7 miles, then turn right (north) on the paved and signed Arizona Snowbowl Road (Forest Road 516). Continue 6.5 miles to the ski area lodge, and turn right into the first parking lot. Drive to the far end of the parking lot and park at the Kachina Trailhead.

The Hike

After hiking up the trail for 0.1 mile, you'll cross under a

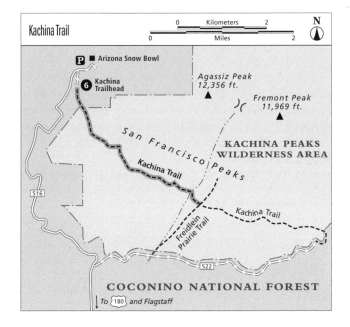

Kachina Trail

0   Kilometers   2

0   Miles   2

N

Arizona Snow Bowl

Kachina Trailhead

6

Agassiz Peak 12,356 ft.

Fremont Peak 11,969 ft.

San Francisco Peaks

Kachina Trail

KACHINA PEAKS WILDERNESS AREA

516

Kachina Trail

Freidlein Prairie Trail

522

COCONINO NATIONAL FOREST

To 180 and Flagstaff

power line and enter the Kachina Peaks Wilderness Area. The trail winds in and out of small canyons and through meadows as it traverses the southwest slopes of Agassiz Peak. The forest here is an attractive mixture of quaking aspen, Douglas fir, and limber pine. In fall, the aspen change to beautiful shades of yellow, orange, and red, and this hike provides a good opportunity to view those colors.

After about 1 mile, you will head across a rocky canyon. Beyond this point, the trail crosses a steeper, more rugged slope. After crossing several small draws, the trail crosses the deeper canyon that comes down from Fremont Saddle, then traverses into Freidlein Prairie, an alpine meadow on the southwest slopes of Fremont Peak. The hike ends at the junction with the Freidlein Prairie Trail at 2.7 miles. Return to the trailhead as you came.

An option for a hike of moderate difficulty is to continue to the east end of the Kachina Trail, which adds 3.6 miles to the total distance of the hike, but only 200 feet of additional elevation change. Allow an extra 2 hours for this option.

Miles and Directions

0.0 Trailhead.

2.7 Reach the Freidlein Prairie Trail junction.

5.4 Arrive back at the trailhead.

7 Lockett Meadow–Waterline Loop

This unique hike features alpine valleys and quaking aspen groves. It provides a fine sample of the glacial and volcanic features of the San Francisco Peaks, and is a great "fall color" hike.

Location: 22 miles northeast of Flagstaff.

Distance: 4.4-mile loop.

Approximate hiking time: 3 hours.

Elevation change: 860 feet.

Best seasons: Summer through fall.

Water: A tap at the watershed cabins is a water source during the summer only. Treat the water before drinking.

Other trail users: Mountain bikes, horses.

Canine compatibility: Dogs are allowed if kept under control.

Permits and restrictions: Cross-country hiking is prohibited above 11,400 feet (approximately timberline). The Interior Valley above Lockett Meadow is closed to all overnight camping to protect the watershed for Flagstaff. For details on this closure, contact the Peaks Ranger District. Maps of the closure area are posted at the trailhead.

Maps: USGS Sunset Crater West and Humphreys Peak; Coconino National Forest.

Trail contacts: Peaks Ranger District, Coconino National Forest, (928) 526-0866. www.fs .fed.us/r3/coconino.

Finding the trailhead: From Flagstaff, drive north on U.S. Highway 89, the main street through town, and continue about 17 miles to Schultz Pass Road (Forest Road 520), and turn left (west). This maintained dirt road is opposite the Sunset Crater National Monument turnoff. Drive 0.4 miles, then turn right at a T intersection. Continue 0.8 mile to another T intersection, and then turn left. About 0.6 mile farther, just before a locked gate at a cinder pit, turn right on the Lockett Meadow Road, Forest Road 522. Continue 2.8 more

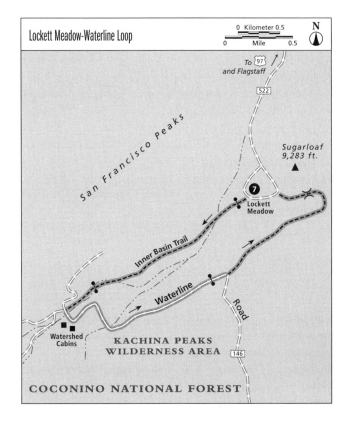

Lockett Meadow-Waterline Loop

0   Kilometer   0.5

N

0   Mile   0.5

To 97
and Flagstaff

522

Sugarloaf
9,283 ft.

San Francisco Peaks

7
Lockett
Meadow

Inner Basin Trail

Waterline   Road

Watershed
Cabins

KACHINA PEAKS
WILDERNESS AREA

146

COCONINO NATIONAL FOREST

miles to Lockett Trailhead at the southwest corner of the one-way
loop road around Lockett Meadow.

The Hike

Follow the Inner Basin Trail (not shown on the topographic
map), which climbs gradually southwest through fine stands
of quaking aspen, ponderosa pine, and the occasional limber
pine. The valley floor is broad and fairly flat, though cut

by numerous small gullies. If you take the time to walk to either side of the valley, you will notice that the bordering slopes are very steep. This is characteristic of valleys carved by glaciers. The moving ice shapes the entire valley into a broad U-shape. Valleys carved entirely by water have a V-shaped cross section.

Another glacial characteristic is the unsorted debris that make up the valley floor. Rocks and boulders of all sizes are randomly scattered about, instead of being sorted by size as they are when carried and deposited by running water. As a glacier moves downhill, it scours rocks from its bed. More rock falls from the slopes above and is carried by the glacier. When the ice melts, the sand, gravel, rocks, and boulders are dropped in an unsorted heap, called "glacial till."

After 1.5 miles, the Inner Basin Trail reaches a small group of watershed cabins at the junction of several roads. During the summer, untreated spring water is available at a tap by the largest cabin. The main cabin serves as an emergency shelter for snow surveyors from the U.S. Soil Conservation Service. Snow surveys are conducted throughout the mountains of the West to predict the amount of snow runoff that will occur in the spring. Such predictions are important because much of the drinking and irrigation water used in the West comes from mountain watersheds. The smaller cabins protect the pipelines that collect water from springs and wells higher in the Interior Valley. The pipelines merge here into one pipe that follows the road upon which you hike.

Turn left and take the Waterline Road (Forest Road 146). The road contours through an especially fine aspen stand as it heads east-northeast along the lower slopes of Doyle Peak. Used to access the watershed project in the Interior Valley, the road is closed to all motor vehicles except those on official business. Generally, traffic is limited to weekdays when an occasional maintenance truck passes by, so this road makes a very pleasant and cool hike. You may also encounter mountain bikes, which are allowed on the San Francisco Peaks except in the Kachina Peaks Wilderness Area, and horses, which are allowed everywhere except in the watershed above the cabins.

At 2.8 miles, the road passes through a gate and turns sharply right as it crosses the east ridge of Doyle Peak. Leave the road and continue east-northeast on an old road that is closed to vehicles down the ridge. The forest abruptly changes to open stands of ponderosa pines as you hike from cool, north-facing slopes to warmer, south-facing terrain.

About 1 mile after leaving the Waterline Road, the old road turns left (northwest) into a saddle next to Sugarloaf, the large cinder cone blocking the lower end of the Interior Valley. Lockett Meadow is visible below to the northwest. You will enjoy excellent views of the Interior Valley as you descend into the meadow. Follow the old road through the saddle and west for another 0.2 mile into Lockett Meadow at 4 miles. Follow the Lockett Meadow loop road left (west) for 0.4 mile to the trailhead.

Miles and Directions

- **0.0**   Lockett Trailhead.
- **1.5**   Reach the watershed cabins and turn left (east) on Waterline Road.
- **2.8**   Turn left and follow the old road northeast down the ridge.
- **3.8**   Reach the saddle next to Sugarloaf.
- **4.0**   Arrive at Lockett Meadow.
- **4.4**   Return to the Lockett Trailhead.

Elden Mountain and the Dry Lake Hills

Elden Mountain is the 9,299-foot mountain rising dramatically above east Flagstaff, between the city and the San Francisco Peaks. The Dry Lake Hills are somewhat lower—the highest point is 8,819 feet. These mountains lie to the west of Elden Mountain, almost directly north of west Flagstaff. They are connected to Elden Mountain by an unnamed, 8,400-foot pass. Schultz Pass, to the north, separates the Dry Lake Hills from the San Francisco Peaks. The USDA Forest Service has developed an extensive network of trails on the Dry Lake Hills and Elden Mountain. Open to all nonmotorized uses, these trails are popular with hikers and mountain bikers alike. Flagstaff is lucky to have such a fine trail system right next to town. The trails interconnect, offering a variety of loop hikes. You can also reach this trail network from Flagstaff via the Urban Trail System.

Camping

There are two public campgrounds within the Coconino National Forest in this area: Bonito Campground near Sunset Crater National Monument, off U.S. Highway 89 on Forest Road 545, and Little Elden Springs Horse Camp, located west of US 89 on Forest Road 556. There are several private campgrounds in the Flagstaff area—see the Flagstaff section for details. Dispersed camping is allowed in the Coconino National Forest unless specifically posted otherwise. Be extremely careful with fire, especially during the summer and fall dry seasons. Campfires are prohibited during periods of high fire danger.

Access and Services

The Dry Lake Hills and the north side of Elden Mountain are reached from Flagstaff via U.S. Highway 180 and Schultz Pass Road, which is paved for the first 0.8 mile and maintained dirt afterward. The east side of Elden Mountain is reached from US 89 north of Flagstaff. Flagstaff has all services available.

$\bigcirc$ 8 Brookbank Trail

This short hike heads up a historic wagon road in the Dry Lake Hills. The hike ends at a seasonal lake and meadow, which is surrounded by a fine mixed forest of aspen, pine, and fir. Close-up views of the San Francisco Peaks are a special bonus.

Location: 6 miles northwest of Flagstaff.
Distance: 2.2 miles out and back.
Approximate hiking time: 2 hours.
Elevation change: 630 feet.
Best seasons: Summer through fall.
Water: None.
Other trail users: Horses and mountain bikes.

Canine compatibility: Dogs are allowed if kept under control.
Permits and restrictions: None.
Maps: USGS Sunset Crater West and Humphreys Peak; Coconino National Forest. The trail is not on the topo map.
Trail contacts: Peaks Ranger District, Coconino National Forest, 5075 N. Highway 89, Flagstaff, AZ 86004, (928) 526-0866, www.fs.fed.us/r3/coconino/.

Finding the trailhead: From Flagstaff, drive 3 miles north on U.S. Highway 180. Turn right (north) on Schultz Pass Road (Forest Road 420). Drive 0.5 mile, then go straight (north) onto the Elden Mountain Road (Forest Road 557), which is a maintained dirt road. Continue past a few houses and through a gate (this gate is closed in winter and spring when the road is muddy). The road becomes rougher but is passable to most vehicles if driven with care. Park at the East Rocky Ridge Trailhead on the right (northeast); the trailhead is 3 miles from the Schultz Pass Road.

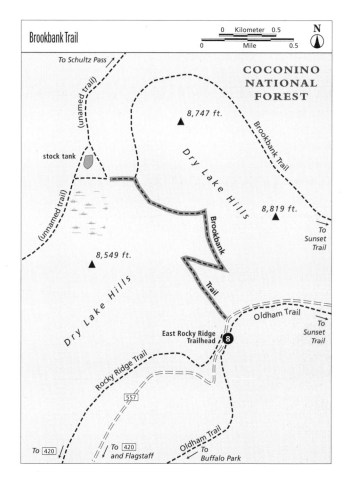

0   Kilometer   0.5

0   Mile   0.5

N

COCONINO
NATIONAL
FOREST

To Schultz Pass

(unnamed trail)

stock tank

8,747 ft.

Dry Lake Hills

Brookbank Trail

8,819 ft.

To
Sunset
Trail

(unnamed trail)

Brookbank

8,549 ft.

Dry Lake Hills

Trail

Oldham Trail

To
Sunset
Trail

East Rocky Ridge
Trailhead   **8**

Rocky Ridge Trail

557

To 420

To 420
and Flagstaff

Oldham Trail

To
Buffalo Park

The Hike

The Dry Lake Hills get their name from several meadows
that lie on the summit plateau. Early in the season, after
the snow melts, the meadows become seasonal lakes. As

the lakes dry up, the meadows in turn become a riot of wildflowers.

The meadow at the end of this hike is on private land. Although there are no restrictions on hiking at present, this could change in the future. Always respect private property and obey all signs, if posted.

Walk a few dozen yards north up Elden Mountain Road to the signed Brookbank Trail. Turn left (northwest) on the trail, which follows an old wagon road up an unnamed canyon, then climbs south-facing slopes via several switchbacks. The old road apparently was built by an early settler to reach the meadows that grace the top of the Dry Lake Hills.

After a moderate but sustained climb through mixed ponderosa pine, Douglas fir, aspen, and Gambel oak forest, with an occasional view to the south, the trail reaches a junction. The Brookbank Trail goes right (north), but this route continues straight ahead on the unnamed trail. You will reach a broad, open meadow at 1.1 mile. The graceful summit of Agassiz Peak, the second highest summit of the San Francisco Peaks at 12,356 feet, looms above the meadow.

Miles and Directions

- **0.0** Trailhead.
- **1.0** Stay left on an unnamed trail where the signed Brookbank Trail goes right.
- **1.1** Reach the dry lake and meadow.
- **2.2** Arrive back at the trailhead.

9 Rocky Ridge Trail

This is an easy hike along the base of the Dry Lake Hills. The trail faces south and dries out earlier in the spring than the other trails in the Dry Lake Hills–Elden Mountain trail system. Access is quick from Flagstaff. This is a good hike when you do not have much time.

Location: 4 miles northwest of Flagstaff.
Distance: 5.4 miles out and back.
Approximate hiking time: 3 hours.
Elevation change: 440 feet.
Best seasons: Late spring through fall.
Water: None.
Other trail users: Horses and mountain bikes.
Canine compatibility: Dogs are allowed if kept under control.
Permits and restrictions: None.
Maps: USGS Flagstaff West, Humphreys Peak, and Sunset Crater West; Coconino National Forest. The trail is not shown on the topographic map.
Trail contacts: Peaks Ranger District, Coconino National Forest, 5075 N. Highway 89, Flagstaff, AZ 86004, (928) 526-0866, www.fs.fed.us/r3/coconino/.

Finding the trailhead: From Flagstaff, drive northwest about 3 miles on U.S. Highway 180, then turn right (north) on the Schultz Pass Road (Forest Road 420). Continue 0.8 mile to the end of the pavement and park near the gate at the Schultz Creek Trailhead. The gate may be closed during winter and early spring when Schultz Pass Road is muddy.

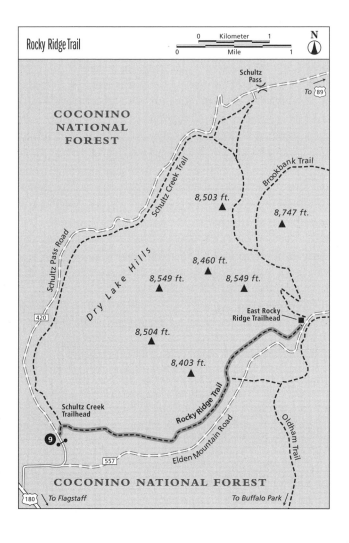

Rocky Ridge Trail

0 Kilometer 1

0 Mile 1

N

COCONINO NATIONAL FOREST

Schultz Pass

To 89

Schultz Creek Trail

Brookbank Trail

8,503 ft.

8,747 ft.

Schultz Pass Road

420

8,460 ft.

8,549 ft.

8,549 ft.

Dry Lake Hills

East Rocky Ridge Trailhead

8,504 ft.

8,403 ft.

Rocky Ridge Trail

Schultz Creek Trailhead

Oldham Trail

9

Elden Mountain Road

557

COCONINO NATIONAL FOREST

180   To Flagstaff

To Buffalo Park

The Hike

Walk through the gate, then down an unmaintained dirt road to the right (northeast) for about 0.1 mile to the signed trailhead. Go right (east) on the Rocky Ridge Trail and follow it up a gentle slope. The trail stays below the steep south slope of the Dry Lake Hills. It climbs gradually through open ponderosa pine and oak forest, and eventually turns more to the north as it enters the canyon between the Dry Lake Hills and Elden Mountain. At 1.2 miles, watch for a metal bearing-tree poster on a pine next to the trail. Forest Service surveyors use bearing-trees, which are marked with small (about 4 inches square) metal posters, to give the direction and distance to a nearby survey marker. One or more bearing-trees serve as backups in the event the primary marker is moved or lost.

The trail continues to contour along the slopes, gradually getting closer to the Elden Mountain Road (Forest Road 557). As the road first becomes visible below, a spur trail branches right (east), descends to Elden Mountain Road, then connects to the Oldham Trail. Remain on the Rocky Ridge Trail, which stays above the road and swings east, then north as the canyon narrows, before ending at the road at 2.7 miles. To return to the trailhead, retrace your steps.

(**Options:** You could continue the hike by heading off onto any of three other trails that leave from the East Rocky Ridge trailhead. See the Brookbank (Hike 8), Sunset-Brookbank Loop (Hike 10), and Oldham (Hike 12) trail descriptions for more details.)

Miles and Directions

0.0 Schultz Creek Trailhead.

1.2 Pass the bearing-tree.

2.7 Arrive at the East Rocky Ridge Trailhead.

5.4 Arrive back at the Schultz Creek Trailhead.

10 Sunset-Brookbank Loop

This hike features easy access to the cool, alpine forest and meadows of the Dry Lake Hills. Most of the hike traverses a shady, mixed forest of Douglas fir, limber pine, ponderosa pine, and aspen, and it also crosses several open meadows with views of the Dry Lake Hills, Mount Elden, and the San Francisco Peaks.

Location: 8 miles northwest of Flagstaff.
Distance: 5.4-mile loop.
Approximate hiking time: 4 hours.
Elevation change: 630 feet.
Best seasons: Summer through fall.
Water: None.
Other trail users: Horses and mountain bikes.
Canine compatibility: Dogs are allowed if kept under control.

Permits and restrictions: None.
Maps: USGS Humphreys Peak and Sunset Crater West; Coconino National Forest. These trails are relatively new and are not shown on topographic maps of the area.
Trail contacts: Peaks Ranger District, Coconino National Forest, 5075 N. Highway 89, Flagstaff, AZ 86004, (928) 526-0866, www.fs.fed.us/r3/coconino/.

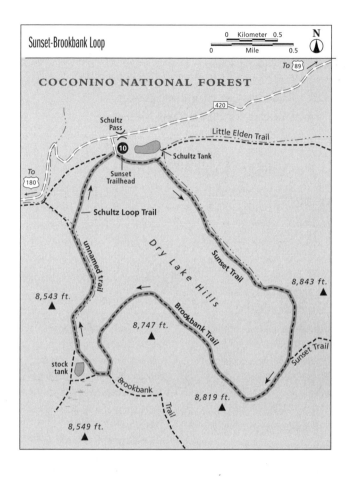

Sunset-Brookbank Loop

0 Kilometer 0.5
0   Mile   0.5
N

To 89

COCONINO NATIONAL FOREST

420

Schultz Pass

Little Elden Trail

10

Schultz Tank

Sunset Trailhead

To 180

— Schultz Loop Trail

unnamed trail

Dry Lake Hills

Sunset Trail

8,543 ft.

8,843 ft.

8,747 ft.

Brookbank Trail

Sunset Trail

stock tank

Brookbank Trail

8,819 ft.

8,549 ft.

Finding the trailhead: From Flagstaff, drive northwest about 3 miles on U.S. Highway 180. Turn right (north) on the Schultz Pass Road (Forest Road 420). Continue past the end of the pavement on the maintained dirt road to the Sunset Trailhead at Schultz Pass, 5.3 miles from the highway.

The Hike

From the trailhead, follow the Sunset Trail as it crosses the gentle slope above Schultz Tank through a beautiful ponderosa pine and aspen forest. The Little Elden Trail goes left (northeast) at 0.2 mile; continue straight (southeast) on the Sunset Trail. The trail enters a small drainage and turns uphill. Climbing steadily but at a moderate grade, the trail stays on the right (west) side of the drainage for more than a mile. It then crosses an old road, veers out of the drainage to the left (east) and enters a more open forest. The open aspect is due to the logging that occurred in the area.

The trail reaches the crest of the Dry Lake Hills at 1.7 miles, where there are good views of the San Francisco Peaks to the north. The trail then descends on the south side of the ridge and heads southwest to meet the Brookbank Trail at 2 miles.

From this junction, continue straight (southwest) on the Brookbank Trail as it follows the contour of the slope westward. Here, the forest is a pleasing mixture of ponderosa pine, Douglas fir, and aspen. Soon the trail crosses over a broad saddle and turns north. It descends though a small meadow, then descends northwest via several switchbacks through dense fir forest. The trail passes through another saddle and meadow, then contours around a hill to the north. The forest is so dense here that there are very few views. Continuing around the hill, the trail heads south, then meets a T intersection at 3.8 miles. Turn right (uphill and northwest) onto the unsigned trail. After a hundred yards, the trail levels out into a large meadow with a seasonal lake, the largest in the Dry Lake Hills.

The next section of trail crosses private land that is open to hikers at present. Please respect private property and all posted signs. At 4.2 miles, the trail follows an old road as it starts across the meadow. Watch for the good trail branching right (north) before the road crosses the meadow. Take this trail directly toward the San Francisco Peaks, skirting a small stock tank on the east. Join an old road just north of the stock tank. Follow the road downhill to the north.

At the junction with Schultz Loop Trail at 4.9 miles, turn right (northwest) and continue to Sunset Trailhead, which is at 5.4 miles.

Miles and Directions

0.0 Sunset Trailhead.

0.2 Stay right (southeast) at Little Elden Trail junction.

1.7 Cross the crest of the Dry Lake Hills.

2.0 Go straight ahead onto Brookbank Trail.

3.8 At the intersection, turn right (uphill) onto an unnamed trail.

4.2 Join an old road below the stock tank, and turn right (downhill).

4.9 Go right (northeast) at the junction with Schultz Loop Trail.

5.4 Arrive back at the Sunset Trailhead.

1 1 Fatmans Loop

This scenic hike travels through rugged terrain on the east slopes of Elden Mountain. This loop trail is accessible via paved roads and, because of its southeast exposure, dries out earlier than other trails at the same elevation.

Location: Northeast Flagstaff.
Distance: 2.2-mile loop.
Approximate hiking time: 2 hours.
Elevation change: 540 feet.
Best seasons: Spring through fall.
Water: None.
Other trail users: Horses and mountain bikes.

Canine compatibility: Dogs must be leashed.
Permits and restrictions: None.
Maps: USGS Flagstaff East; Coconino National Forest.
Trail contacts: Peaks Ranger District, Coconino National Forest, 5075 N. Highway 89, Flagstaff, AZ 86004, (928) 526-0866, www.fs.fed.us/r3/coconino/.

Finding the trailhead: From the junction of Interstate 40 and U.S. Highway 89 in east Flagstaff, drive north on US 89 about 0.6 miles, then turn left (west) into the Elden Mountain Trailhead parking area. This trailhead is just north of the Peaks Ranger Station.

The Hike

This trail traverses some rugged volcanic terrain with good views. From the trailhead, follow the trail past the information sign and through a gate. Turn left (northwest) at the first signed junction at 0.2 mile; this is the start of the Fatmans Loop. You will return on the trail that forks to the right. The trail climbs northwest toward the imposing

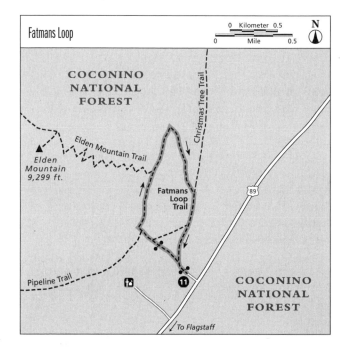

To Flagstaff

east face of Elden Mountain. It passes through another gate where an unsigned trail joins from the right. At 0.4 mile, you'll pass the Pipeline Trail, which goes left (southwest). Continue on the Fatmans Loop as it turns north and climbs the lower slopes of the mountain through Gambel oak and ponderosa pine forest.

At the high point of the loop, the Elden Mountain Trail goes left (west) at 0.8 mile. Stay right on the Fatmans Loop as it continues north, then abruptly turns southeast and starts to descend, winding through huge volcanic boulders.

As it comes out onto the lower, gentler slopes, the trail meets the Christmas Tree Trail, which joins on the left (northeast) at 1.6 miles. Continue to the right (south) to the Fatmans Loop junction at 2 miles, then turn left (southeast) to return to the trailhead.

Miles and Directions

0.0 Elden Mountain Trailhead.

0.2 Turn left (northwest) at the start of Fatmans Loop.

0.4 At the Pipeline Trail, stay right (north).

0.8 At the junction with the Elden Mountain Trail, stay right (north).

1.6 At the Christmas Tree Trail crossing, stay right again.

2.0 Reach the end of Fatmans Loop and turn left (south).

2.2 Arrive at the Elden Mountain Trailhead.

Flagstaff

The present site of Flagstaff received attention from early American explorers because of the presence of several good springs. These were a vital water source in an otherwise dry landscape. In 1851, a party under U.S. Army captain Lorenzo Sitgreaves passed through the area south of the San Francisco Peaks; in 1859, construction started on the Beale Wagon Road. Intended as an immigrant route to California, the Beale Road was used to reach Prescott after gold was discovered there in 1863.

In 1876, a migrant party camped a few miles southeast of the San Francisco Peaks. They celebrated the one hundredth anniversary of the signing of the Declaration of Independence by stripping a large ponderosa pine to use as a flagstaff, which gave the tiny settlement its name.

When the transcontinental railroad was completed in 1883, Flagstaff began to grow, primarily as a lumbering and ranching town. Later, America's first transcontinental highway, Route 66, was built across northern Arizona and through Flagstaff.

Today, Flagstaff is a busy commercial center at the junction of five major highways and the railroad. Flagstaff's economy depends primarily on tourism, Northern Arizona University, several research institutions, and some light industry. At 7,000 feet, it is the highest city of its size in the country and is surrounded by the Coconino National Forest. The city is developing an extensive urban trail system, which is open to hikers, bicyclists, and other nonmotorized users.

Camping

There is one public campground near the city—Fort Tuthill County Park Campground, located just south of town on Interstate 17 at the airport exit. Private campgrounds include KOA Flagstaff on N. U.S. Highway 89, Black Bart's RV Park on Butler Avenue east of Interstate 40, and Woody Mountain Campground on W. Old Route 66. Dispersed camping is allowed in the Coconino National Forest unless specifically posted otherwise. Be extremely careful with fire, especially during the summer and fall dry seasons. Campfires are prohibited during periods of high fire danger.

Access and Services

The trails in the city area are all reached via paved streets, and the city has all visitor services, including several outdoor shops that sell hiking gear.

12 Oldham Trail

This trail along the base of Elden Mountain provides access to the Dry Lake Hills–Elden Mountain trail system from Flagstaff. It crosses a portion of McMillan Mesa, which offers expansive views of the San Francisco Peaks, the Dry Lake Hills, and Elden Mountain, before skirting the base of Elden Mountain through volcanic boulders and shady mixed forest.

Location: In Flagstaff.
Distance: 6.2 miles out and back.
Approximate hiking time: 4 hours.
Elevation change: 540 feet.
Best seasons: Summer and fall.
Water: Water is available at the trailhead in the summer.
Other trail users: Horses and mountain bikes.

Canine compatibility: Dogs must be on leashes in Buffalo Park.
Permits and restrictions: None.
Maps: USGS Flagstaff West and Humphreys Peak; Coconino National Forest.
Trail contacts: Peaks Ranger District, Coconino National Forest, 5075 N. Highway 89, Flagstaff, AZ 86004, (928) 526-0866, www.fs.fed.us/r3/coconino/.

Finding the trailhead: This hike is located in the north-central section of the city, adjacent to the Coconino National Forest. From the junction of U.S. Highway 180 and Business 40 (Route 66), drive north on US 180 (Humphreys Street) to Columbus. Turn right (east), go one block, then turn left (north) on Beaver Street. Continue to Forest Street, then turn right (east). Continue for 0.8 mile on Forest Street, then turn left (west) at the sign for Buffalo Park and the U.S. Geological Survey Astrogeology Center. Follow the road for 0.2 mile to its end at the Buffalo Park Trailhead.

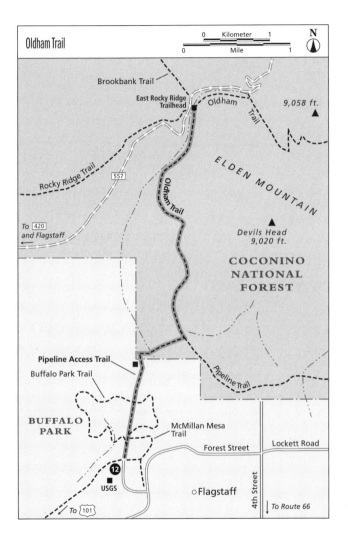

Oldham Trail

0   Kilometer   1
0   Mile   1

N

Brookbank Trail

East Rocky Ridge
Trailhead

Oldham Trail

9,058 ft.

Oldham Trail

Rocky Ridge Trail

557

ELDEN MOUNTAIN

To 420
and Flagstaff

Devils Head
9,020 ft.

COCONINO
NATIONAL
FOREST

Pipeline Access Trail

Buffalo Park Trail

Pipeline Trail

BUFFALO
PARK

McMillan Mesa
Trail

Forest Street

Lockett Road

12

USGS

4th Street

Flagstaff

To 101

To Route 66

The Hike

To begin, go through the old gate into Buffalo Park. Continue north on the Pipeline Access Trail, which goes to the gas pipeline station at the north side of the park. At 0.6 mile and the park boundary, the Oldham Trail starts just to the right (east) of the buildings, at a gap in the fence. The trail descends the slopes of the mesa, then heads northeast across the shallow valley below, directly toward Elden Mountain. Numerous false trails go both left and right in this area.

The Oldham Trail meets the signed Pipeline Access Trail at 1.5 miles on the north side of the cleared gas pipeline right of way. Turn left (north) on the Oldham Trail and climb gradually along the west slopes of Elden Mountain. The Dry Lake Hills are visible to the northwest, and soon it is obvious that the trail is heading into the canyon between the Dry Lake Hills and Elden Mountain. After a short descent, you will pass an unmarked trail coming in from the left (west). Make note of this junction and avoid taking this false trail by mistake on the return.

Though the views are limited, the pine-oak forest and the volcanic boulders make this an interesting hike. Fir and aspen begin to mix with the pine as you near the northern end of the trail about 3 miles from the start, and the slopes to the right (east) become a rock cliff. At 3.1 miles, you will reach the signed East Rocky Ridge Trailhead on the Elden Mountain Road. This is also the parking area for a very popular rock climbing area.

This hike ends at the East Rocky Ridge Trailhead, but you can extend your hike by continuing on the Oldham Trail, or hiking on the Brookbank Trail (Hike 8), or the Rocky Ridge Trail (Hike 9).

Miles and Directions

0.0 Buffalo Park Trailhead.

0.6 Reach the start of the Oldham Trail at the park boundary.

1.5 At the Pipeline Access Trail junction, stay left (north).

3.1 Arrive at the East Rocky Ridge Trailhead, your turnaround point.

6.2 Arrive back at the Buffalo Park Trailhead.

13 Buffalo Park

Located on Switzer Mesa, this popular, easy walk is part of the Flagstaff Urban Trail System. The scattered pine forest and open meadows give this place a special feeling. The spaciousness is enhanced by the great views of the San Francisco Peaks, the Dry Lake Hills, and Elden Mountain.

Location: In Flagstaff.

Distance: 2-mile loop.

Approximate hiking time: 1 hour.

Elevation change: None.

Best seasons: Spring through fall.

Water: Water is available at the trailhead in the summer.

Other trail users: Mountain bikes.

Canine compatibility: Dogs must be on leashes in Buffalo Park.

Permits and restrictions: None.

Maps: USGS Flagstaff West. Though Buffalo Park is shown on the topographic map of this area, the Buffalo Park Trail is not.

Trail contacts: City of Flagstaff Parks and Recreation, 211 West Aspen Avenue, Flagstaff, AZ 86001, (928) 779-7690, http://flagstaff.az.gov/.

Finding the trailhead: From the junction of U.S. Highway 180 and Business 40 (Route 66), drive north on US 180 (Humphreys Street) to Columbus. Turn right (east), go one block, then turn left (north) on

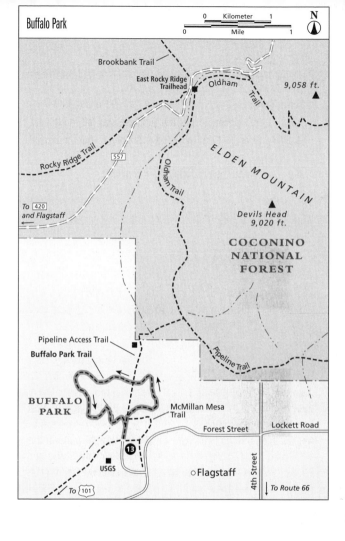

Buffalo Park

Brookbank Trail

East Rocky Ridge
Trailhead
Oldham
Trail

9,058 ft.

Rocky Ridge Trail

557

ELDEN MOUNTAIN

Oldham Trail

To 420
and Flagstaff

Devils Head
9,020 ft.

COCONINO
NATIONAL
FOREST

Pipeline Access Trail

Buffalo Park Trail

Pipeline Trail

BUFFALO
PARK

McMillan Mesa
Trail

Lockett Road

Forest Street

13

4th Street

USGS

Flagstaff

To 101

To Route 66

Beaver Street. Continue to Forest Street, then turn right (east). Continue on Forest Street for 0.8 mile, then turn left (west) at the sign for Buffalo Park and the U.S. Geological Survey Astrogeology Center. Follow the road for 0.2 mile to its end at the Buffalo Park Trailhead.

The Hike

Buffalo Park was originally developed by the city of Flagstaff to hold a small herd of buffalo. The high fences, roads, and entrance station were built so that people could drive through the park and view the buffalo. In the late 1960s the buffalo were moved to a state buffalo range, and the facilities were abandoned. Since then, the park has become popular with hikers, walkers, mountain bikers, and runners. In the late 1980s, the park narrowly escaped having a major road built through it, but that proposal was soundly rejected by a citizens' initiative—proving that the people of Flagstaff greatly value and appreciate the remarkable views and serenity of this elevated mesa within the city.

The U.S. Geological Survey Astrogeology Center is located just south of the trailhead. Data from unmanned spacecraft is analyzed here and used to create maps and photos of other planets. In the 1960s, moon-bound astronauts trained here and amid the volcanic hills and craters around Flagstaff.

To begin, walk through the entrance gate, then continue north. Pass the McMillan Mesa Trail, then turn right (east) at the next fork, which is the outer loop trail. Stay on this trail as it does a loop more or less around the perimeter of the park. At 0.8 mile, you will cross the Pipeline Access Trail, which runs north through the park and leads to the Oldham Trail (Hike 12). Taking this right (north) turn leads you onto the national forest trail system on the Dry Lake

Hills and Elden Mountain. Or, you can turn left (south) for a shortcut back to the trailhead. Otherwise, follow the trail straight (west) as it loops through the park back to the trailhead.

Miles and Directions

0.0 Trailhead.
0.8 Cross the Pipeline Access Trail.
2.0 Return to the trailhead.

14 Observatory Mesa Trail

An easily accessible day hike on the Flagstaff Urban Trail System, the Observatory Mesa Trail also provides access to the Coconino National Forest.

Location: In west Flagstaff.
Distance: 3.2 miles out and back.
Approximate hiking time: 2 hours.
Elevation change: 400 feet.
Best seasons: Summer through fall.
Water: None.
Other trail users: Mountain bikes.
Canine compatibility: Dogs are allowed if kept under control.

Permits and restrictions: Much of the trail crosses private land owned by Lowell Observatory; hiking off the trail is not permitted.
Maps: USGS West Flagstaff; Coconino National Forest.
Trail contacts: City of Flagstaff Parks and Recreation, 211 West Aspen Avenue, Flagstaff, AZ 86001, (928) 779-7690, http://flagstaff.az.gov/.

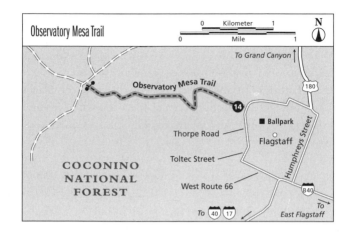

Finding the trailhead: From the intersection of Business 40 (Route 66) and U.S. Highway 180 (Humphreys Street), drive west on Route 66. Continue straight ahead onto Santa Fe Avenue; do not go under the underpass. Continue several blocks, then turn right (north) on Toltec Street, which becomes Thorpe Road. Pass the Adult Center building, which is on the left (west), and watch for the baseball field on the right (east). The best parking for the trail is the baseball field parking lot.

The Hike

Observatory Mesa is named for Lowell Observatory, which is located on its southeast rim. Percival Lowell established the observatory in 1894, just a few years after the settlement of Flagstaff. The combination of railroad access and the clear mountain air provided an ideal location for observing the stars and planets.

An influx of astronomers and other researchers began to change the character of the small logging town. Much notable research has been done at the observatory—the most famous of which was the discovery of the planet Pluto in the early 1930s. Today, Lowell is one of a small worldwide network of observatories searching for asteroids that cross Earth's orbit and could conceivably strike the planet. Currently, research continues in cooperation with Northern Arizona University and the nearby U.S. Naval Observatory. Tours and exhibits are available at the observatory visitor center.

The trail actually crosses through the ballpark area from the east, but this hike picks up the trail on the west side of Thorpe Road where a sign marks the Urban Trail System. A map of the trail system is also posted here. The Observatory Mesa Trail goes west through the city park, then follows a gully west. Watch for bicycles, especially on the steep downhill sections. The trail turns left (south) at 0.4 mile and climbs steeply out of the gully to reach the top of Observatory Mesa at 0.6 mile. From here, the trail turns west again and continues through the pine forest. At 1.6 miles, the trail ends at a gate and a junction with several forest roads. It is possible to use these roads for an extended hike; refer to the topographic map and the Coconino National Forest map for more information.

Miles and Directions

0.0 Begin at the baseball field.

0.4 The trail climbs south out of the canyon.

0.6 Reach the top of Observatory Mesa and head west.

1.6 The trail ends at a gate.

3.2 Arrive back at the baseball field.

15 Arizona Trail on the Walnut Canyon Rim

This long and scenic hike follows a section of the Arizona Trail along the north rim of Walnut Canyon. Walnut Canyon is a tributary of the Little Colorado River, with its headwaters at Upper Lake Mary. Crossing Arizona from Utah to Mexico through some of Arizona's most wild and scenic country, more than 750 miles of the 800-mile Arizona Trail have been completed. The Arizona Trail Association plans to celebrate the completion of the trail in 2012, the one hundredth anniversary of Arizona statehood.

Location: 8 miles southeast of Flagstaff.

Distance: 13.6 miles out and back.

Approximate hiking time: 7 hours.

Elevation change: 280 feet.

Best seasons: Summer through fall.

Water: None.

Other trail users: Horses and mountain bikes.

Canine compatibility: Dogs are allowed if kept under control.

Permits and restrictions: None.

Maps: USGS Flagstaff East; Coconino National Forest.

Trail contacts: Peaks Ranger District, Coconino National Forest, 5075 N. Highway 89, Flagstaff, AZ 86004, (928) 526-0866, www.fs.fed.us/r3/ coconino/; Arizona Trail Association, www.aztrail.org.

Finding the trailhead: From the junction of Interstate 40 and U.S. Highway 89 in Flagstaff, drive 4 miles east on I-40 to the Walnut Canyon National Monument exit, and go right (south). Continue 2.5 miles, then turn right (west) on Old Walnut Canyon Road (Forest

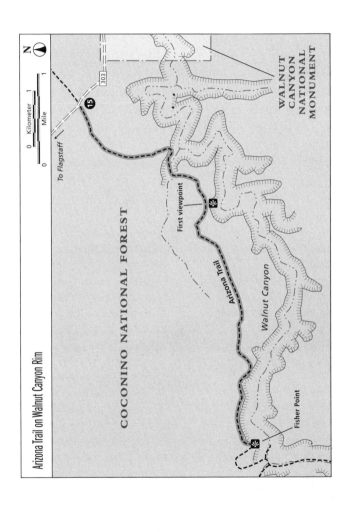

Arizona Trail on Walnut Canyon Rim

N

0   Kilometer   1
0   Mile   1

To Flagstaff

303

15

COCONINO NATIONAL FOREST

First viewpoint

Arizona Trail

Walnut Canyon

Fisher Point

WALNUT
CANYON
NATIONAL
MONUMENT

Road 303), which is just before you enter the monument. Continue for 1.8 miles to the Arizona Trail parking area.

The Hike

This hike follows a finished section of the Arizona Trail, which when complete will cross the entire state from Utah to Mexico. Parts of the trail follow old roads, while other sections are new trail construction. Pay close attention to the trail markers; the trail is not shown on the USGS topographic map of the area.

The trail starts off by heading southwest through an open ponderosa pine–Gambel oak forest, and climbs gradually. It turns south, then joins an old road for a short distance. New trail construction takes you across a side canyon at 1.9 miles. On the far side, the path joins another old road.

Watch for a spur trail on the left (south). It goes to a viewpoint overlooking Walnut Canyon at 2.4 miles. After the viewpoint, the trail follows old roads for more than one mile, and wanders away from the rim.

The trail leaves the road again, then hits the north rim of Walnut Canyon at 5.5 miles. The route follows the rim closely all the way to Fisher Point at 6.8 miles. This viewpoint, reached by a few yards of spur trail, overlooks the point where the canyon makes an abrupt ninety-degree change in direction. It makes an ideal goal for a hike on this portion of the Arizona Trail.

From Fisher Point, you can also hike south on the Arizona Trail and exit via the Sandys Canyon Trail (Hike 16), or even continue to the Arizona Trail trailhead at Marshall Lake. Both these options require a car shuttle. See the Sandys Canyon and Arizona Trail across Anderson Mesa (Hike 17) trail descriptions for details.

Cliff dwellings and artifacts, relics of the Sinagua people who thrived in this area around a thousand years ago, are common in Walnut Canyon. The canyon provided protection from enemies, as well as shelter from the worst of the summer heat and winter weather. For more information on the Sinagua, pay a visit to Walnut Canyon National Monument by continuing south on Walnut Canyon Road from I-40. There is also a paved nature trail at the visitor center, which loops around a promontory jutting out into the canyon, passing a number of well-preserved Sinagua ruins.

Miles and Directions

0.0 Trailhead.
1.9 Cross a side canyon.
2.4 Reach the first Walnut Canyon viewpoint.
5.5 The trail reaches the Walnut Canyon rim again.
6.8 Arrive at Fisher Point.
13.6 Arrive back at the trailhead.

Lake Country

Despite the 100 inches of snowfall it receives each year, most of the Coconino Plateau lacks surface water because of the porous limestone and volcanic rock that underlies the plateau. The area southeast of Flagstaff is an exception, and is known locally as the Lake Country because of its numerous small lakes. Most are shallow, while others have been augmented with artificial dams. The lakes are remnants of the wet period during the last glaciation, which ended about 10,000 years ago. Many of the natural meadows that occur throughout the Flagstaff area are dry lake beds, some of which briefly hold water after wet winters. These meadows have dense soil, formed from silt deposited in the former lake, which makes it difficult for ponderosa pines to take root. The forest very slowly reclaims the meadows, spreading inward from the edges. Three of the hikes in this section are near Mormon Lake, the largest natural lake in Arizona and a haven for wildlife.

Camping

There are numerous public campgrounds in the Coconino National Forest southeast of Flagstaff. Lake View and Pine Grove Campgrounds are near Upper Lake Mary, off Forest Highway 3 (Lake Mary Road). Ashurst Lake and Forked Pine Campgrounds are east of Forest Highway 3 on Forest Road 82E at Ashurst Lake. Dairy Springs and Double Springs Campgrounds are located near Mormon Lake, west of Forest Highway 3 on Forest Road 90. The Ledges Trail (Hike 19) starts from Dairy Springs Campground, and the Lake View Trail (Hike 20) starts from Double Springs Campground. Dispersed camping is allowed in the Coconino National Forest unless specifically posted otherwise. Be extremely careful with fire, especially during the summer and fall dry seasons. Campfires are prohibited during periods of high fire danger.

Access and Services

The Lake Country is reached via Lake Mary Road (Forest Highway 3), a paved road running southeast from Flagstaff. Limited services are available at Mormon Lake Village. Full services are located in Flagstaff.

16 Sandys Canyon Trail

This hike near Lower Lake Mary offers interesting geology, views, and a connection to the Arizona Trail.

Location: 7 miles southeast of Flagstaff.

Distance: 2.8 miles out and back.

Approximate hiking time: 2 hours.

Elevation change: 200 feet.

Best seasons: Spring through fall.

Water: None.

Other trail users: Horses and mountain bikes.

Canine compatibility: Dogs are allowed if kept under control.

Permits and restrictions: None.

Maps: USGS Flagstaff East; Coconino National Forest. The trail is not shown on the topographic map.

Trail contacts: Peaks Ranger District, Coconino National Forest, 5075 N. Highway 89, Flagstaff, AZ 86004, (928) 526-0866, www.fs.fed.us/r3/coconino/.

Finding the trailhead: From Flagstaff, drive south on Milton Road, then turn right (west) on Woodlands Village Drive (this junction is signed for Lake Mary). Go one block, then turn left (south) on Beulah Street. Continue 0.6 mile, then turn left (southeast) on Lake Mary Road (Forest Highway 3). Drive 5.7 miles, then turn left (east) just after crossing a cattle guard. This unsigned gravel road leads into an unnamed, informal campground. Bear left (northeast) and continue to the signed trailhead at the northeast corner of the campground.

The Hike

The first section of the trail follows an old road leading directly toward the rim of upper Walnut Canyon, which is visible ahead. At the rim at 0.7 mile, the trail turns left

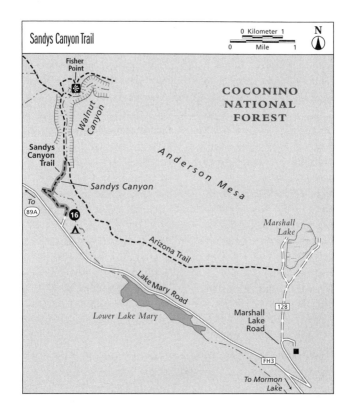

0 Kilometer 1

0 Mile 1

N

COCONINO NATIONAL FOREST

Fisher Point

Walnut Canyon

Sandys Canyon Trail

Sandys Canyon

Anderson Mesa

To 89A

16

Arizona Trail

Marshall Lake

Lake Mary Road

Lower Lake Mary

Marshall Lake Road

128

FH3

To Mormon Lake

(north) and skirts the edge of Sandys Canyon, a tributary of Walnut Canyon. The ponderosa pine forest here is open and spacious, and views of Walnut Canyon are only a few steps to the east. At one point there is an outcrop of volcanic rock on the rim and a massive boulder field cascading into the canyon. On the opposite wall of the canyon, the horizontal strata of the Kaibab limestone form white cliffs. The Kaibab limestone is the uppermost layer of sedimentary rock on the Coconino Plateau and forms both the south and north rims of the Grand Canyon. In much of the Flagstaff area however, it is covered with lava flows.

The trail crosses a shallow drainage, then turns sharply right (east) and descends Sandys Canyon. A sign marks this spot. A few aspen trees, wild grapevines, and stands of poison ivy can be found during the short descent to the floor of Walnut Canyon. Poison ivy is a small plant that has shiny green leaves growing three to a bunch. It is usually found near or in streambeds, but not necessarily with flowing water. Many people suffer a serious rash and even blisters from contact with poison ivy. Fortunately, it is easy to spot because it grows in association with wild grape. The grapevines here are a tangled mass of low growing vines and leaves, and the poison ivy grows as single plants.

After the trail crosses the (normally dry) bed of Walnut Creek at 0.9 mile, it turns left (north) and follows a former Jeep road up the canyon bottom. The canyon floor is broad and open. After about 0.5 mile, the trail emerges into a meadow and ends at the junction with the Arizona Trail at 1.4 miles. It is worth turning right (south) and walking a few steps to another fine meadow and an impressive cliff of Coconino sandstone. Also found in the Grand Canyon, Coconino sandstone was formed from wind-drifted sand dunes, and the cross-bedded layers of sand are still visible in the rock today.

Return to the trailhead by retracing your steps along Sandys Canyon Trail.

(**Options:** You can continue the hike either north or south on the Arizona Trail. See the Arizona Trail on the Walnut Canyon Rim (Hike 15) and the Arizona Trail across Anderson Mesa (Hike 17) descriptions for details.)

Miles and Directions

0.0 Trailhead.

0.7 Skirt the rim of Sandys Canyon.

0.9 Cross Walnut Canyon.

1.4 Meet the Arizona Trail.

2.8 Arrive back at the trailhead.

17 Arizona Trail across Anderson Mesa

This hike starts in a good wildlife viewing area and traverses a section of the Arizona Trail across Anderson Mesa to a scenic viewpoint overlooking Walnut Canyon.

Location: 8 miles southeast of Flagstaff.

Distance: 11.6 miles out and back.

Approximate hiking time: 6 hours.

Elevation change: 490 feet.

Best seasons: Spring through fall.

Water: None.

Other trail users: Horses and mountain bikes.

Canine compatibility: Dogs are allowed if kept under control.

Permits and restrictions: None.

Maps: USGS Lower Lake Mary and Flagstaff East; Coconino National Forest. The trail is not shown on the topographic maps.

Trail contacts: Peaks Ranger District, Coconino National Forest, 5075 N. Highway 89, Flagstaff, AZ 86004, (928) 526-0866, www.fs.fed.us/r3/coconino/; Arizona Trail Association, www.aztrail.org.

Finding the trailhead: From Flagstaff, drive south on Milton Road, then turn right (west) on Woodlands Village Drive (this junction is signed for Lake Mary). Go a block, then turn left (south) on Beulah Street. Continue 0.6 mile, then turn left (southeast) on Lake

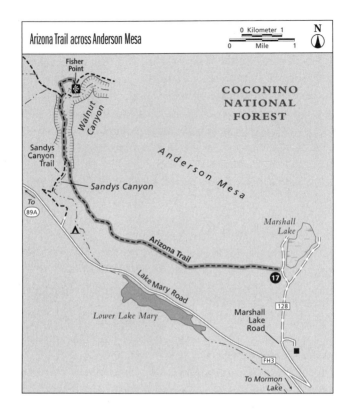

Arizona Trail across Anderson Mesa

0 Kilometer 1
0 Mile 1

N

Fisher Point

COCONINO NATIONAL FOREST

Walnut Canyon

Sandys Canyon Trail

Anderson Mesa

Sandys Canyon

To 89A

Arizona Trail

Marshall Lake

17

Lake Mary Road

128

Lower Lake Mary

Marshall Lake Road

FH3

To Mormon Lake

Mary Road (Forest Highway 3). Drive 9.9 miles, then turn left (east) on the paved, signed Marshall Lake Road. After about a mile, the paved road turns sharply right (east)—continue straight (north) on the signed, maintained dirt road (Forest Road 128) to Marshall Lake. When the meadow containing the shallow, marshy lake comes into view, turn left (northwest) at a fork, then watch for the small sign marking the Arizona Trail at a parking area on the left (northwest).

The Hike

You will start near the shore of Marshall Lake, which is usually more of a marsh than a lake. Because of the excellent cover, it is a good place to view waterfowl and other wildlife; the best times are before sunrise and after sunset. The trail starts from the small sign at the parking area and heads west through the open pine-oak-juniper forest on Anderson Mesa. The trail climbs gradually, then crosses a small canyon at 1.3 miles, one of the many tributaries of Walnut Canyon. You'll cross several smaller drainages before reaching the rim of Walnut Canyon at 3 miles.

The trail gradually descends into Walnut Canyon itself. There are good views of the San Francisco Peaks to the northwest and occasional glimpses into Walnut Canyon as you hike. A single switchback leads to the bottom of the canyon, where it reaches the junction with the Sandys Canyon Trail at 4 miles. Turn right and continue north down Walnut Canyon. The walking is especially pleasant through a series of meadows.

Abruptly, the canyon makes a sharp right (east) turn. At 4.9 miles, a trail leaves the canyon to the northwest; turn right (northeast) to stay on the Arizona Trail. After 100 yards, the Arizona Trail turns left and goes up a small side canyon to the north. Do not continue on the unnamed trail down Walnut Canyon by mistake. The Arizona Trail climbs out of the side canyon on the east, then swings southeast to Fisher Point at 5.8 miles. This fine viewpoint overlooking Walnut Canyon is the destination for this hike.

Retrace your steps to the trailhead.

(**Options:** With a car shuttle, you could use the Sandys Canyon Trail to make this a one-way hike. See the Sandys

Canyon Trail (Hike 16) description for information. Or, you could continue on the Arizona Trail past Fisher Point to the Walnut Canyon Trailhead; see the Arizona Trail on the Walnut Canyon Rim (Hike 15) trail description for details.)

Miles and Directions

0.0   Trailhead.

1.3   Cross a shallow canyon.

3.0   Rim of Walnut Canyon.

4.0   At the junction with the Sandys Canyon Trail, stay right (north).

4.9   Turn right, then almost immediately left, to stay on the Arizona Trail.

5.8   Reach Fisher Point.

11.6   Arrive back at the trailhead.

18 Mormon Lake

This is a level hike that goes along the shore of Mormon Lake, Arizona's largest natural lake and a great place to view wildlife.

Location: 27 miles southeast of Flagstaff.
Distance: 6.4 miles out and back.
Approximate hiking time: 3 hours.
Elevation change: None.
Best seasons: Spring through fall.
Water: None.
Other trail users: Horses and mountain bikes.

Canine compatibility: Dogs are allowed if kept under control.
Permits and restrictions: None.
Maps: USGS Mormon Lake; Coconino National Forest.
Trail contacts: Peaks Ranger District, Coconino National Forest, 5075 N. Highway 89, Flagstaff, AZ 86004, (928) 526-0866, www.fs.fed.us/r3/coconino/.

Finding the trailhead: From Flagstaff, drive 27 miles southeast on Lake Mary Road (Forest Highway 3). The highway skirts the east side of Mormon Lake, then descends through a road cut. Watch for the turnoff to Kinnikinick Lake on the left (east), then turn right (west) onto an unmarked, unmaintained dirt road that descends toward the lake, then turns right (north). Go through the gate (low-clearance cars should be parked at the gate). Drive to a fork; turn right (uphill) and drive a few yards to a second gate and park. This gate is normally locked to protect the area's wildlife.

The Hike

Most of the year, Mormon Lake is more a marsh than a lake. When full, after the spring snowmelt, it is the largest

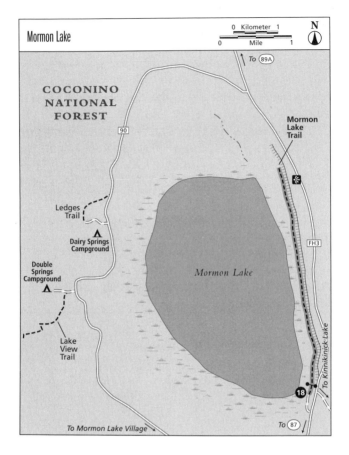

To 89A

COCONINO
NATIONAL
FOREST

90

Mormon
Lake
Trail

Ledges
Trail

Dairy Springs
Campground

Double
Springs
Campground

Mormon Lake

FH3

Lake
View
Trail

To Mormon Lake Village

To Kinnikinick Lake

18

To 87

"natural" lake in Arizona. Although there is no dam (in contrast with Upper and Lower Lake Mary), humans have still influenced the lake. The area was first settled by Mormons, who started dairy farming here. In the pioneer days, the lake area was never more than a marsh, and the settlers ran cattle on the rich forage. Eventually, the hooves of the cattle compacted the soil and made it less porous, so that the marsh flooded and became a lake in wet years. Today, the lake and its marshes are important havens for wildlife.

This walk follows the old road along the shore of the lake. The topographic map shows this old road, but not the present highway, which is to the east, above the lakeside cliffs.

The old road is nearly level and is about 20 feet higher than the lake, so there is a good view. This hike is best done at sunrise or sunset, which are good times for wildlife viewing. The old road can be followed more than 3 miles along the eastern shore, to a point just past the viewpoint on the new highway at 3.2 miles. Cottonwood and aspen trees grow here in an unusual association, and there are fine views of the distant San Francisco Peaks.

Retrace your steps to the trailhead.

Miles and Directions

0.0 Trailhead.

3.2 Reach the north end of old highway.

6.4 Back at the trailhead.

19 Ledges Trail

This is a very easy hike to a vantage point near Mormon Lake. This is another good location for wildlife viewing.

Location: 22 miles southeast of Flagstaff.
Distance: 1.2 miles out and back.
Approximate hiking time: 1 hour.
Elevation change: 100 feet.
Best seasons: Spring through fall.
Water: None.
Other trail users: Horses and mountain bikes.

Canine compatibility: Dogs are allowed if kept under control.
Permits and restrictions: None.
Maps: USGS Mormon Lake; Coconino National Forest.
Trail contacts: Peaks Ranger District, Coconino National Forest, 5075 N. Highway 89, Flagstaff, AZ 86004, (928) 526-0866, www.fs.fed.us/r3/coconino/.

Finding the trailhead: From Flagstaff, drive about 27 miles south on Lake Mary Road (Forest Highway 3), then turn right (west) on the Mormon Lake Road (Forest Road 90). Continue for 3.6 miles, then turn right (west) into Dairy Springs Campground. Drive through the campground to site 26 and the trailhead.

The Hike

This well-defined trail traverses the hillside above a row of summer homes, climbing gradually for about a half a mile. It then descends to a small ledge at 0.6 mile, where you will enjoy a view of the north end of Mormon Lake. Although the Mormon Lake Road is just a short distance away, the pavement is nicely hidden in the trees, and the view of the

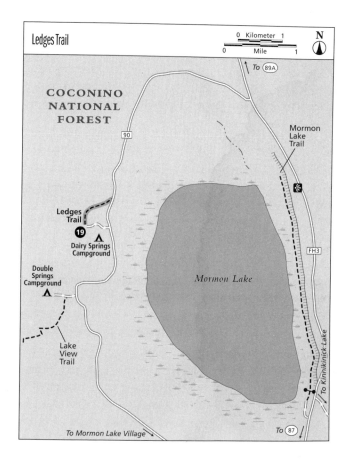

lake from this vantage point is nearly unspoiled. This is a great place to watch wildlife, as the ledge is about 100 feet above the lake. Bring binoculars, and plan to arrive around sunrise or before sunset for the best viewing.

The trail continues to a private camp. It is best to return the way you came.

Miles and Directions

0.0 Trailhead at site 26.

0.6 Reach the viewpoint.

1.2 Arrive back at site 26.

20 Lake View Trail

This pleasant hike offers expansive views of Mormon Lake and the surrounding ponderosa pine forest.

Location: 28 miles southeast of Flagstaff.

Distance: 2.8 miles out and back.

Approximate hiking time: 2 hours.

Elevation change: 500 feet.

Best seasons: Spring through fall.

Water: None.

Other trail users: Horses and mountain bikes.

Canine compatibility: Dogs are allowed if kept under control.

Permits and restrictions: None.

Maps: USGS Mormon Lake and Mormon Mountain; Coconino National Forest. The trail is not shown on the topographic map.

Trail contacts: Peaks Ranger District, Coconino National Forest, 5075 N. Highway 89, Flagstaff, AZ 86004, (928) 526-0866, www.fs.fed.us/r3/coconino/.

Finding the trailhead: From Flagstaff, drive about 27 miles south on Lake Mary Road (Forest Highway 3), then turn right (west) on the Mormon Lake Road (Forest Road 90). Continue for 5 miles, then turn right (west) into Double Springs Campground. The trailhead is signed and is on the left side of the road along the south side of the campground.

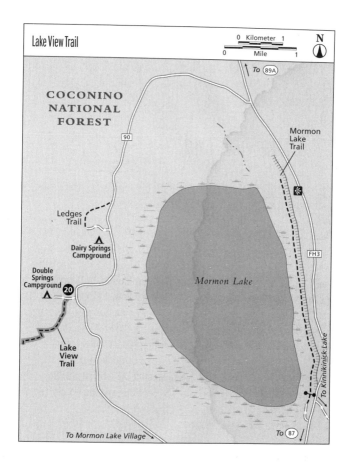

Lake View Trail

COCONINO
NATIONAL
FOREST

To 89A

Mormon
Lake
Trail

90

Ledges
Trail

Dairy Springs
Campground

Double
Springs
Campground 20

Lake
View
Trail

Mormon Lake

FH3

To Kinnikinick Lake

To Mormon Lake Village

To 87

0   Kilometer   1

0   Mile   1

N

The Hike

The Lake View Trail climbs gradually along a shallow drainage through pine-oak forest for about 1 mile, then switchbacks up a hill to the rim of a rock outcrop. It works along the outcrop for about 0.2 mile to a point at 1.4 miles that has a commanding view of the ponderosa pine forest and the south end of Mormon Lake. The lake is about a mile away, so the view is not as intimate as that from the Ledges Trail, but the location feels more remote.

Miles and Directions

0.0 Trailhead at Double Springs Campground.

1.4 Reach the viewpoint.

2.8 Arrive back at the campground.

About the Author

Bruce Grubbs has been hiking, cross-country skiing, paddling, biking, and climbing in the Southwest for more than thirty years. He is a writer, photographer, and active charter pilot.

His other FalconGuides include:

Basic Essentials: Using GPS
Best Easy Day Hikes Sedona
Best Hikes Near Phoenix
Camping Arizona
Desert Hiking Tips
Explore! Joshua Tree National Park
Explore! Mount Shasta Country
Grand Canyon National Park Pocket Guide
FalconGuide to Saguaro National Park and the Santa Catalina Mountains
Hiking Arizona
Hiking Arizona's Superstition and Mazatzal Country
Hiking Great Basin National Park
Hiking Northern Arizona
Hiking Oregon's Central Cascades
Mountain Biking St. George and Cedar City
Mountain Biking Flagstaff and Sedona
Mountain Biking Phoenix